# How to Sell Auto and Home Insurance.
## Second Edition

A guide to qualifying, presenting and closing.

By Michael Bonilla

Copyright 2019

## About the Author.

Believe it or not this section is always the hardest for me to write about. I really don't enjoy talking about myself. I enjoy having people talk about themselves. What do people want to know about an author? Background? Experiences? Belief systems? I enjoy breaking things and putting them back together. What kind of person am I? What kind of person do I want to represent?

Let me tell you a brief story that tells you what kind of person I am. Back in the early 90's I was sketching out my design for a boxcar derby car for boy scouts. This was my first race and I couldn't think of the type of car I wanted to build. To say the least there was zero inspiration. I scribbled out some designs on this piece of paper and eventually after running out of paper went into the den to find more paper. I stopped for a second and glanced over by the window. Then it hit me.

What if I used my father's truck as the design? I re-read the instructions and rules for the derby. The boxcar kit came in a small cardboard box with a block of wood we could use to make our cars. The instructions read as follows:

- Must have 4 wheels
- Must weigh X LBs, no more and no less.
- Must be X inches long by X Inches wide.

So, that being said. Nowhere in the rules/instructions did it specifically say "this boxcar must be a car". So, for the first time in boxcar derby history. Michael Bonilla entered a truck into the race. To which everyone started overwhelmingly laughing. It was a small wooded version of a 1990's Dodge Ram 2500. With a big Pepsi decal on the driver side door. So, we called it the Pepsi truck.

I placed my 'car' on the race line for the first race and hoped for the best. The judges looked at it. It met the weight requirements, the size requirements and had the appropriate amount of wheels. So, we raced and I waited with anticipation for the results. As I was short I couldn't even see the race. All I heard was, "Pepsi truck 1st place." After all 5 races that day I kept hearing those same words over and over again.

After sweeping that year's event. The following year I decided to change it up and make a replica of the Mach 5 Speed Racer Car, in which I came in third place. That next year every 'car' was a truck, besides mine. Don't bend the rules, don't break the rules, test the rules and test the boundaries of the game you are given. Look for loopholes and exploits in the system.

I'm unsure what kind of insight that story might have provided. Nevertheless, this book is the longest, most thorough and probably well thought out I have written to date. I'm an author, a consultant, a former agency owner, an avid golfer, a husband and most importantly someone who enjoys giving back through teaching.

**Forward**

This book is a supplement to, "How to Sell Property and Casualty Insurance. And, "How to Start and Build an Insurance Agency: An Insurance Agency and Brokerage Guidebook." This book touches on actual processes for selling auto and home insurance. Most of these processes are geared towards selling to preferred markets with little or no recent claims history.

As you develop your practice you will have to make a decision. Where is your time best spent? Is it best spent competing against an online direct writing insurance company with a $1,000,000,000 marketing budget and low prices or is best spent filtering clients and figuring out where you play and who you play well with? If you want to transition from transactional selling based on price to actual value based selling and consultative selling, this book is a great starting guide.

We often get caught up in the muck and mire of running an insurance agency. The phone rings and a mortgage company needs an updated EOI yesterday and so on and so forth. It's nice to take some time and take a step back to think about what we do, rather than just think about what we have to do.

As always with my books, please mind the grammar. This book like all of my books are sales books, it's not War and Peace. The value of this book is in the system and the process. Please enjoy and take in as much as you can.

## Table of Contents

About the Author. .................................................................. 4

Forward .................................................................................. 8

Chapter 1: Introduction ..................................................... 18

    Who will this system help? ........................................... 21

    What does it mean to be an insurance agent? .... 22

    What does it take to sell insurance? ....................... 23

    The Processes in This Book. ....................................... 24

    Limited Information ........................................................ 25

    Sales Modality .................................................................. 26

    Q.E.R.C. Sales Process .................................................. 27

        Question ........................................................................ 28

        Educate .......................................................................... 28

        Recommend ................................................................. 28

        Close with a question. ............................................. 29

    H.A.U.L. System ............................................................... 29

    Why Do People Talk to Agents? ................................. 31

    Offer a solution not a price, present on value. ..... 31

    Personal Risk Manager Approach ............................ 33

Chapter 2: Qualification & Opening .............................. 36

    Qualification: Opening Questions Setting the Pace ........................................................................................... 37

Typical responses to Opening Questions. ..............38

An often overlooked follow up question. ...............39

Another often overlooked follow up question. .....39

Pivoting from the Answer. ...........................................41

Qualification: Client Identification and Segmentation ...................................................................42

    Client Identification .................................................42

    Client Segmentation................................................43

    Price Shoppers .........................................................43

    Bargain Shoppers.....................................................44

    Convenience Shoppers............................................44

    Relationship Shoppers.............................................44

    Coverage Shoppers .................................................45

    Vengeance Shoppers ..............................................45

    First Time Consumers..............................................46

Identifying a Price Shopper.........................................46

Identifying Bargain Shoppers.....................................47

Identifying Convenience Shoppers...........................47

Identifying Relationship Shoppers............................48

Identifying Coverage Shoppers .................................48

What do all of these consumers have in common? ...............................................................................................49

Have you heard of the S.T.A.R system? (Personality Types)........................................................50

- S. Stability .................................................. 50
- T. Technical .................................................. 51
- A. Action ..................................................... 51
- R. Relationship .............................................. 52

Slick Statements .............................................. 52

Think People vs Feel People ................................... 53

Understand Consumer Life Stages ............................... 53

Who is a Prospect and who is a Suspect? ....................... 54

Qualification: Rapport Building ............................... 55

But, Mike what if I'm not interesting? ........................ 56

Qualification: Fact Finding ................................... 57

Qualification: Explain your process ........................... 58

Well, Mike aren't most people too busy to come in the office? ................................................. 60

Qualification: Understanding the current insurance. ................................................... 62

Qualification: Foreshadowing .................................. 62

Chapter 3: Identify Weaknesses and Gaps in current offer. .................................................. 67

- Problem Identification ....................................... 67
- Upselling Water-Backup Sewer and Drainage ................... 69
- Transitioning Questions ..................................... 70
- Don't make up a prospects mind for them. ................... 70
- Inferring Micro Agreements .................................. 71

    The Goal of a Sales Person ............................................. 72

    Typical Weaknesses ........................................................ 72

Chapter 4: Customize a solution based on that information. ................................................................................. 75

    Explain the coverage line by line. ................................. 76

    Explain the Endorsements ............................................. 77

    Checking Rapport ........................................................... 77

    Put the power in the hands of the consumer. ........... 78

    Who is in the home? ...................................................... 79

    Leveraging Fair Rental Value ......................................... 80

    Closing the Show. ........................................................... 80

Chapter 5: Auto Insurance Case Study ........................... 83

    What are your initial thoughts when reviewing this policy? ................................................................................. 83

    Does this client have enough insurance in California? ................................................................................ 84

    What did the agent do right? ........................................ 84

    How do we know if a client has enough insurance? Do the math. ............................................................ 85

    Two Facts for Liability Coverage .................................. 86

    But, Mike I don't drive much anymore… ................... 87

    Addressing Property Damage ...................................... 87

    Common Mistakes Agents Make ................................. 89

    Selling Medical Payments Coverage ........................... 91

    Question to open............................................................92

    Educate ...........................................................................93

    Recommendation ...........................................................94

    Question to Close ..........................................................94

Chapter 6: Home Insurance Case Study....................97

    What are your initial thoughts after reviewing this policy? ............................................................................97

    When I look at the above Dec page here is what I see... .................................................................................99

    $1000 vs $2500 on a home deductible. ..................99

    Instead why not try this................................................101

    Upselling Low Liability Limits....................................102

    Jewelry Sublimit ............................................................104

    Low Medical Payments to Guests/Others.............104

    Extended Replacement Cost Coverage.................105

    Current RCT vs Policy Written RCT. .......................106

    Demand Surge and the RCT .....................................107

Chapter 7: Mindset..............................................................110

    Me, Myself and I ............................................................112

Chapter 8: Goal Setting....................................................114

    Goal Setting Example (Reverse Sales Funnel)...114

    Vision .................................................................................117

Chapter 09: Closing ...........................................................119

My thoughts on Closing ............................................. 119

Closing Strategies .................................................... 120

Closing Statements ................................................. 120

Stop, Look and Listen .............................................. 120

Chapter 10: Objections ................................................. 123

Types of Objections ................................................. 123

    No Time .............................................................. 124

    No Money ........................................................... 124

    No Need .............................................................. 125

    No Trust .............................................................. 125

Rebuttals ................................................................. 125

Why do people object? ........................................... 126

Complaint vs Objection ........................................... 127

Flight, Fight or Freeze ............................................ 128

Chapter 11: Sales Rules/Tips ........................................ 130

Rule Number 1: Don't Complicate Something Simple. ................................................................... 130

Rule Number 2: Always be agreeable. .................... 131

Rule Number 3: Understand the Person. ............... 132

Rule Number 4: The Prospect Needs to understand you. ...................................................... 133

Rule Number 5: Reciprocity ..................................... 134

Rule Number 6: Stick to a process. ........................ 135

Rule Number 7: Know When To Close and Know When to Fold. ..................137

Rule Number 8: Ask Open Ended Questions ......139

Rule number 9: Set Expectations ..........................140

Rule Number 10: Don't lose control of the conversation. ................................................141

Rule Number 11: Don't always try to reinvent the wheel. .......................................................142

Rule Number 12: Speak in Future Tense..............143

Rule Number 13: Ask for Permission to Ask for the Sale. ....................................................144

Rule Number 14: Don't Present Price Present a Solution. ..................................................145

Rule Number 15: Put yourself in a position to win. ..........................................................146

Rule Number 16: Dance through the pain ..........147

Rule Number 17: Have a Personal Story .............147

Index of Questions .........................................149

Summation ...................................................151

Other Books ..................................................152

"The only true wisdom is in knowing you know nothing." - Socrates

## Chapter 1: Introduction

Are you selling on price or on value? Most people reading this book will probably say something to the extent of, "I'm a coverage merchant first, then we focus on price." Or, "We always present on value." Either way... this is a system for upselling limits, upselling deductibles, selling preferred and standard risks for auto and home insurance, based purely on value and not price.

*Michael Jans posted a study on his website (AgencyRevolution.com), in which he stated that, '57% of independent agency customers don't take the lowest quote. In fact, his research has shown that the majority of customers actually take quotes that are 19 to 53% more in premium.'*\*

Why is that? Because, people have different concerns and wants during the buying process. For instance, some client's want an

Agent to take care of everything and are willing to pay a little more. Some people want to have the Agent as a backup for E&O purposes, because the consumer doesn't want to make a mistake when buying. For example, if you go out and buy insurance from a direct writer and don't know the exclusions or gaps and have a claim that is excluded... who pays for it? How many people know the difference between a named owner policy and a full permissive use policy? How many consumers understand the loss severity of water backup sewer and drainage? How many consumers properly understand sub-limits or demand surge? How many consumers understand how subrogation works in regards to choosing a deductible? People also have different value systems. Some people see a price that is too good to be true and understand that not all insurance is created equally.

Why is this important to know? You cannot go Apples to Apples against a direct writer as a broker or as a captive Agency owner. You just can't win or won't win often. Direct writers have niched out the sub-standard market for auto insurance, but have struggled to gain a real foothold on the property market. Occasionally you can win but, if customers are willing to take higher quotes why not quote apples to Oranges. This has always been my operating theory when selling insurance. Most customers share similar characteristics:

1. They don't know what they have.
2. They don't know what they need.
3. They see misleading price comparisons on TV and from other Agents.
4. They don't know if their current insurance is up to date or protects their assets.
5. Most Agents make mistakes.

## Who will this system help?

In my practice most of the consumers we put on the books were preferred clients with multiple policies. We focused on consumers with a low rates of incidences and little or no major violations along with low home claim occurrence. Initially we had the idea that everyone who walked in the door was a prospect. What we found was that the consumers who didn't value insurance or value protecting their assets didn't fit well with our agency.

We focused on higher liability limits, we focused on customizing the policy to fit the needs of each risk, but most of all we spent time to understand the person we were speaking with. We moved people from 15/30 to 250/500 quite often. Maybe not 57% of the time, but more often than you would think. The reason we focused on value selling is the fact we never wanted to lose a carrier appointment because of loss ratios, because we've seen it happen. If you tend to make people money they keep you around, in the case of insurance companies keeping your loss ratio below 55%. In our case we had a combined loss ratio over 20 companies of around 35%.

What does it mean to be an insurance agent?

Have you ever taken the time to think about this question? Why do people need us? What do we do? Why are we valuable? If you can't answer these questions, then how can you sell your service to consumers? Once, ironically a financial services guy asked me, "Why do we even need insurance agents?" To which I replied, "Well, you can let an algorithm run your financial portfolio or a person you trust, it's the same thing right?" People can do their taxes online, get medical advice from WebMD instead of a doctor, there are many activities that can be outsourced to the internet of things. Ultimately, our job is advise. Advise on the right policy for the right risk, we are market makers and pair the right company to the right client. We educate on the likelihood and consequences of an evolving risk portfolio. As you progress through stages of your life, your risk changes and so do your insurance needs.

What does it take to sell insurance?

I couldn't tell you how often I've heard agents tell me, 'insurance is a commodity' or 'once my company has better rates I'll start to invest in marketing'. Do you think the direct writers (internet companies) will wait out a hard market cycle to invest in marketing? When I was a broker I made the choice to assume my prices were going to be higher. Why? Because, I was attempting to sell high density accounts from any angle. If you walked in with a home Dec page you were walking out with an auto, home and umbrella policy.

What does it take to sell insurance? It depends on your ability to hold a conversation. A conversation in which you ask open ended questions, spend time understanding the person's wants and needs, a combination of slick statements and well timed factoids.

### The Processes in This Book.

This book is going to break down the selling process into three distinctive parts. We do three things, we Qualify, Identify and Customize. We properly qualify a client and understand their needs/wants, we identify gaps/exposures/problems facing a client and then we customize our presentation and offering to suit their needs.

Most of the questions we are going to ask our big picture to small picture. Along with that we threw in some open ended questions and some questions to direct the conversation. We want to ask a lot of questions that ask to ask. We are asking permission to ask them a question some times.

### Limited Information

Selling in many ways is like poker. Poker is classified as a limited information game and selling for the most part is very similar in that respect. In poker you get two cards and those cards have what is called an implied odds of winning. The longer you play the hand the more information you gather to help make an informed decision. Just like selling insurance.

What are the two cards most prospects get dealt? Price and Coverage. Most prospects are trained by television ads with animals or price-gauging brokers to only discuss price and have short conversations. If you are a trusted advisor you need to play your hand. Discuss needs, wants, concerns, flush out questions, understand the client, provide facts and figures (where appropriate), empathize, explain your process, explain your reason for why you do what you do, customize the offering and do a proper needs analysis!

What I always ask of salespeople is to front load the process. Take some time to be detailed and really understand the client. Put your cards on the table, so to speak. Can the customer make an informed decision if all I bothered to do was quote apples to apples based on their Dec page? No, they cannot. Our job is not to merely educate a client but rather to exchange ideas.

## Sales Modality

How do you sell? Over the phone? Over text? Over Email? In person? Whatever it is make sure you remain consistent. When people send an email normally they want an email back. But, that doesn't mean they will not take the time to sit down with you in person. Part of our job as agents is to properly handle the field underwriting. If we fail to do that we open the flood gates of attractive nuisance and the direct writers to come in and take over.

## Q.E.R.C. Sales Process

During our sales process we are going to learn to sell each coverage feature to a client by using this simple process. This is the process that I used, it's simple and to the point. This process is designed to get the insured to make the decision and critically think about insurance.

1. Question to Open (Transition question and or coverage concern question)

2. Educate about the coverage and risk. (Exposure, likelihood and consequence of risk.)

3. Recommend the coverage amount. (As your agent, based on your risk I recommend...)

4. Close with a question. (Put the ball in the court of the consumer, make them think about it.)

Question

I noticed that you didn't have any Water-Back Up Sewer and Drainage Coverage, can I ask why?

Educate

Explain the Hazard, Gap. Use a story or claims severity information.

Recommend

This is where you make your professional recommendation. As your agent...

Close with a question

Is that something you want coverage for?

## H.A.U.L. System

The H.A.U.L is a simple way to think about presenting and transitioning through product lines. As a multi-line agent we can choose to recommend multiple policies or a single policy per sale. The H.A.U.L system is as simple as presenting with Home Insurance, transitioning to Auto insurance, then cross-selling to Umbrella and presenting a life policy.

Why did I decided to sell insurance this way? For starters, my goal as an agent was to maximize the size of each account. Why? Because, the more policies per client the longer retention of that client. Why? Consumer studies back this fact up, but think about it from a consumer standpoint. How often would you like to shop if you had to provide information on several policies, as opposed to a single policy? Also, I was betting against my competition. Most agents when they receive an auto insurance quote request just quote an auto policy. I would go for 4 policies over 1, even if my close ratio was lower, in the end my workload was drastically lower.

This strategy was rather simple, sandwich the consumers most prized assets. Start with the home, which can be a highly customizable policy. Lever the benefits on the home policy and compare the differences from the current offering. Auto insurance at least in California is all pretty much the same and somewhat of a price game. Transition to umbrella insurance after auto and focus on protecting assets. After you close the commitment for the umbrella insurance, focus on the most prized asset in a persons' life... their family.

## Why Do People Talk to Agents?

When a consumer reaches out to an agent or a company, why do they do it? Because, they need insurance? Wrong! They have a problem they are attempting to solve. Sometimes they think their problem is overpaying for insurance. More often than not the underlying problem is uncertainty or clarity of value. They don't know why they should be paying what they are paying? Why? Because, we don't do a great job of hitting 100% of our yearly insurance reviews or communicate the importance of having good insurance. Every commercial is exactly the same, 'You can save 100% in 10 minutes by switching to LARGE Insurance Co." How are you going to be different?

Offer a solution not a price, present on value.

What is my job as your agent? Is my job

to gloss over the coverages and try to beat the price? Is my job to copy, quote and prey? As your agent my job is to assess your risk, what is the likelihood of a risk, what are the consequences of that risk? How do we protect your assets against that risk? Right? Let's say you are a new homeowner and you need insurance. Owning a home opens up new exposures to risk from hazards. This proposal **WE** are putting together is a customized solution meant to hedge against the consequences of risk by transferring it to the insurance company and not your grandkids. My job is to dig and find out information, what do you know about what the customer knows? What have you heard about claims, about companies and or about me? What are your concerns? What kind of questions might you have about your insurance? My job is to get you in front of me, so we can actually show you the risks surrounding your life. We are experts and advisors, we need to take this seriously and ask for a face to face appointment. Gather the information on the phone and put together two proposals. A proposal for what they asked for and a proposal for what you think they need based on your professional recommendation. An Apples to Apples and Apples to Oranges.

## Personal Risk Manager Approach

My approach to selling and consultations customers on insurance was rather simple. Think of me like your personal risk manager. Firstly, we figure out what kind of assets you have exposes to loss. Secondly, we figure out what kind of hazards are presented given your risk profile. Thirdly, we can then talk about the consequences and likelihood of risk given your specific situation. We look at issues effecting the client and how those can lead to incidents and how we can prevent those incidents from becoming losses and or mitigating or transferring those losses to the insurance company.

"Our greatest weakness lies in giving up. The most certain way to succeed is always to try just one more time." - Thomas A. Edison

## Chapter 2: Qualification & Opening

Qualifying a client is somewhat of a lost art form. Let's break it down into a simple process. So, what is qualifying? Qualifying involves but is not limited to the following factors:

*What does a client care about?*

*Client Identification and Segmentation*

Rapport Building

Fact Finding

Understanding Current Insurance

Explain your process

Foreshadowing – speaking in future tense and setting expectations

## Qualification: Opening Questions Setting the Pace

The questions you ask and how you ask them will dictate a lot of the sale. Here are some easy big picture opening questions:

- How can we help?

- What brings you by today?

- Thanks for stopping by, what's on your mind?

- Before we get started what kind of questions and concerns do you have?

- When was the last time they sat down with their agent and discussed their needs?

All these questions are designed to get the prospect talking and flush out two things. I want to know why they are here and what they care about or what their value systems are.

Typical responses to Opening Questions.

- We'll I'm looking for a lower price.
- I haven't really looked at my insurance in a while.
- I'm shopping around...
- I think I am paying too much.
- I feel I am paying too much.
- I don't feel like I have enough insurance or the right insurance.

Whatever the response you will get a glimpse into a prospect's thinking. This is how we can add value. Most people use price as factor when making a purchasing decision. I'd be lying if I said price wasn't a factor, but what do you buy when you buy insurance? Do you buy a price or do pay a price to purchase peace of mind?

An often overlooked follow up question.
- How did you hear about us?
- Oh by the way John who referred you?

Another often overlooked follow up question.
- What do you care about? (with insurance)
- What else do you care about besides price?
- Why are you looking (NOW) for new insurance?
- Have you ever had to use your insurance?
- Has anyone sat down and explained you how your coverage is supposed to work?
- When was the last time?

All my clients are unique but they all tend to have the same three overarching concerns.

Those concerns are price, coverage and claims service.

- Will I get a fair price for what I need? (Price)
- Will I have enough coverage to protect my family? (Coverage)
- Will the insurance company pay my claim? (Claims)

For the most part this seems like common sense, but it's not common practice. If you're claim gets denied then what's the point of paying for insurance at all.

Agent: "When is the worst time to know you have the wrong policy? Before or after a claim takes place?"

Prospect: "After!"

If you are having trouble getting a client to focus on the value of insurance, why not try just asking? Out of those three categories which is most important to you? Is it having your claim paid in the event of an accident? Is it having enough coverage to protect your family? Or is it your monthly payment? We need to flush out concerns to really add value! See what the prospect prioritizes.

Pivoting from the Answer.

How you pivot will be determined by the responses you are getting. Is the customer solely focused on price? Does the customer have price flexibility? Are they shopping because of a bad experience? Figure out the reason and the client.

## Qualification: Client Identification and Segmentation

### Client Identification

Client identification is simple. There are two types of people. There are 'think' type of people and 'feel' type of people. Some people respond well to stories and some people respond well to facts and numbers. So, how do we figure out who is who? Simple. We ask questions and listen to responses which in turn will help us tailor our message. People tend to respond consistently to your questions. For instance, a feel person will simply say, "I feel that..." And a think person, "I think that..." You cannot use the same sales script on every person and expect it work every time. You are going to have to make adjustments during your presentation.

## Client Segmentation

For Client Segmentation there are 7 or 8 types of insurance shoppers, Price Shoppers, Bargain Shoppers, Convenience Shoppers, Relationship Shoppers, Coverage Shoppers, First Time Consumers, and Vengeance Shoppers. These are categories in my firm we put each client into. Once we knew who we were dealing with, it was easier to tailor our presentation to suit their specific needs or know whether or not to refer them to another firm.

## Price Shoppers

Usually (but not always) a customer in the sub-standard market, higher claims frequency, usually does not understand how insurance works, shops frequently, lower deductibles, etc.

## Bargain Shoppers

You'll find these shoppers in any market. Typically they have lower claims frequency but are looking to save money for equal or better coverage.

## Convenience Shoppers

Some consumers understand the value of insurance but have policies that are scattered all over the place. They might have so many polices that they do not know what they have exactly. They are looking to simplify and will pay more for it. Other convenience shoppers just want to know as their agent you will 'take care of them'. As their agent they want you to make their life easier.

## Relationship Shoppers

These shoppers shop because of an existing relationship. These people usually fall into the category of people who also just want to be cared about. Remember caring is a hot commodity. People love to be around people who care about them.

### Coverage Shoppers

Coverage shoppers have assets or aspire to one day have assets and want protection. They want certainty that a claim if filed will be paid and that they are paying for the protection. They understand the value of insurance and appreciate education.

### Vengeance Shoppers

These shoppers had a bad experience with a claim, a bad experience with billing or the insurance company and or a bad experience with their agent.

### First Time Consumers

A first time buyer could be a spouse who lost a spouse through passing or divorce and now they have to handle the insurance. A young married couple are first time home buyers. Younger clients who have to purchase insurance for the first time.

### Identifying a Price Shopper

Agent: How can we help?

Prospect: "I want/need to pay less for insurance."

Agent: Okay, besides price what do you care about?

Prospect: "I just want the cheapest insurance possible."

### Identifying Bargain Shoppers

Agent: How can we help?

Prospect: "I (think or feel) that I'm paying too much for insurance."

Prospect: "We've been reviewing our budget and think we are looking for areas to save."

Agent: Great. The fastest way to save money with insurance is by looking at slightly higher deductibles. How about we bump up your collision from $500 to $1000?

### Identifying Convenience Shoppers

Agent: How can we help?

Prospect: I've got a lot of insurance and would like to see what's out there.

Agent: Well, let me ask you something Bob, if I could find a way to bundle all of your policies, would that be something you would consider paying a little more for that?

Prospect: Yes, but obviously it depends on how much.

### Identifying Relationship Shoppers

These are friends, family or Co-workers. Maybe a neighbor. Someone who feels that they have somewhat of an obligation to shop based on knowing the Agent.

### Identifying Coverage Shoppers

Agent: What brings you by today?

Prospect: I'm not sure I have the proper amount of coverage.

Agent: Okay, why do you feel that way? Or better yet when was the last time your Agent reviewed your coverage?

Prospect: When I first signed up 10 years ago.

What do all of these consumers have in common?

They are looking for you to solve a problem. The price consumer wants you to provide a cheaper price, the bargain shopper a better value, the convenience shopper to make their life easier, the relationship shopper has an obligation to shop based on an existing relationship and the vengeance shopper just wants you to move.

## Have you heard of the S.T.A.R system?
### (Personality Types)

STAR is a relatively simple way of identifying personality types of different clients (not sure who created this system). Along, with understanding buying motivations (Segmentation), preferences to facts/figures/numbers or stories (Think vs Feel People), you also have to consider personality types when you build a process.

### S. Stability

Stability people thrive on structure and control. Think of Bruce Willis in Armageddon, "I don't trust anyone else to get the job done (but himself)." Most often Do-it-yourselfers. Occupations that thrive on process of structure.

## T. Technical

Technical people prefer illustrations, explanation and exposition. Engineers, professors, data people, etc.... What are the charges? Explain why this policy has a $5 fee built into when no other auto policy does. Let me read the prospectus cover to cover and have 5 or 6 specific policy jacket questions.

## A. Action

Action people make quick decisions with a lot of gut reaction or intuition. Go with your gut. I'm an action person. These people once you can identify them are the opposite of the technical people. Get to the point. Salespeople and business owners fall in to this category. Leaders who lead by example.

## R. Relationship

Relationship People are focused on trust throughout the process. These are the kind of people that like to be wined and dined. People who like to focus on rapport building. Who am I dealing with? They want to be certain about doing business with you.

### Slick Statements

- There is no such thing as a good deal for the wrong insurance policy.
- Would you feel safe purchasing a car knowing it had a faulty airbag?
- It's called umbrella insurance because like an umbrella I'd rather have one and not need it then need one and not have one.
- It really does me no good to sell you a policy that does you no good.

## Think People vs Feel People

I've always liked to categorize clients into to buckets for how I distribute information. People generally speaking fall into one of these two categories. People do really well with perceiving information thru either stories or fact/figures/data.

## Understand Consumer Life Stages

Insurance Shoppers as well as having communication style preferences and differing personality types and different distribution preferences, they also can be bracted into different segments based on stages in life.

- Recent College Graduate – Someone who has little or no insurance experience. Possibly moved back in with parents or living on their own.

- Nuclear Family – typical family structure for the last 50 years.

- Empty Nester – Family with recent kids out of the home.

- Sandwiched Family – three generation household

- Pre-retiree – family before Medicare eligibility but maybe just works part time.

- Retired – possibly someone who is downsizing or hopefully traveling more.

### Who is a Prospect and who is a Suspect?

The biggest mistake I made as a broker and agent was thinking that everyone I spoke with was a prospect. It's tempting because we can sell so many different lines of insurance and when you first start you need to make money. I'm a strong believer that the generalist insurance agency model has more or less run its course. IN the future consumers are going to look for specific experts in lines of insurance. This will become more evident as the direct writers and the online insurance companies gain more steam. So, as we evolved our practice we decided to specialize. This comes back to the question, "What do you do really well?

## Qualification: Rapport Building

How do we build rapport? Let me ask you something. What do we need to know to qualify and write a proper policy? We need to know about a person's family, their occupation, do they volunteer, do they have pets and do they have multiple generations under one roof? Talk about what is interesting to a person and what a person cares about. Hobbies and recreational activities always help because it helps us understand the risk. Caring in itself is a very selfless activity, everyone likes to be around people that we care about and people that care about us.

But, Mike what if I'm not interesting?

This is the problem that most people struggle with when networking or prospecting in social settings. If you are not interesting or don't know how to become interesting start by just becoming interested in other people. We all have the same favorite topic, ourselves. Until we have kids, then the topic shifts a little bit for most people. Keep these questions in mind when prospecting or building rapport.

- What do you do for a living or hobby?
- How long have you been doing that?
- How did you get into that?
- What do you do really well?

- What do you like about what you do?

## Qualification: Fact Finding

Fact finding involves all the questions we need for rate and the rest of the qualifying process involves all of the questions we need to 'right-sell' aka upsell coverage and properly insure the risk. These are some questions to think about in no specific order.

1. Are you married or single?
2. Who's in the household?
3. Who is your current insurance company?
4. How long have you been with that company?
5. When was the last time you had a claim? How was the experience?
6. Do you have any valuable antiques, guns, silverware, etc…

Qualification: Explain your process

My favorite question in the world... **What do you do really well?** The reason why this is my favorite question, is the fact that most people never take the time to think about the answer. And every time I ask this question I can tell based on their facial expression that they have never thought of this question.

When you are contemplating how to explain your process think of this question as it is the most important question for determining the kind of person you want to be. The kind of person you want to represent to the world. The kind of change you want to produce. When someone walks away from a presentation how will they describe me?

When I sell insurance or when I advise multi-million dollar agencies and brokerages I have one goal in mind. My job is not to tell them how to think or what to think, my job is to just give them something to think about.

We do three things in this agency. We educate our clients on their insurance needs, we build a custom offering and then make our professional recommendation based on their needs.

We Qualify, Identify and Customize the coverage…

When you figure out your process or a process that you like to use, figure out a simple way to explain that process to a client. Every person sitting across from you must know, like and trust you. So, this is the know part and the trust part. What does Mike do well? What does he do? How does he do it? Why does he do it? What are you extremely good at? Is the customer 100% certain in my abilities?

Is part of your process to sit down and

explain the coverage or actually do field underwriting? If so, use that. Did you ask the client to sit down or did they email you and you assumed they would not come to the office.

> Well, Mike aren't most people too busy to come in the office?

There is only one way to find out. Ask. Most people don't review insurance information at work anyways they go home and review it. Why not be there to actually answer questions and add value? What most people forget is that the internet has only really been changing our purchasing decisions for about 15 years. Most people still think they have to physically go somewhere and sign an application.

Did you know that 75% of people shop for insurance online to gather information? But, most still buy from non-online companies or non-direct writing companies. Most millennials buy online now. Why is that? Because, we are not asking them to come to the office. Remember college students have all the free time in the world to come to your office as most do not have full time jobs. I'm a millennial (1988) and I worked full time while attending college. Trust me, people my age care, but you have to give us a reason to care. In my firm we focused on face to face business. We sold 75% of all of our clients face to face. The only customers we did not were people that we could not drive to within 2 hours one way or leads from mortgage officers. Most people reading this book would never consider buying insurance online because we all have heard the horror stories of what happens when you do.

## Qualification: Understanding the current insurance.

How well does the insured know what they have? Do they know what is covered and what is not covered? Most of the time the answer is that they do not know or what very little idea of what is covered. Our job is to find out.

## Qualification: Foreshadowing

The most overlooked part of selling is the assumptive close. Or in other words talking as if you already closed the sale.

As your agent...

"As your Agent part of my job is making sure this insurance stays current to protect your assets. How often would you like to meet to review your insurance? Once or twice a year?"

Don't tell every client that you will sit down each year to do an insurance review, give them options. Each client is different. You want to emphasis that you are customizing the offering and thinking of the client for their individual situation. This is all about setting the proper expectations.

As your agent when you have a claim. The first thing that you do is call me. Why? Because, I am your advisor. **Sometimes it's not in your best interest to file a claim.** This requires a good understanding of subrogation and the claims process, so please if you go that route be well versed. My point is not that you set this specific expectation with clients but that you set some expectations.

As your agent I know price is important to you, your human, but what you'll find is that in a major accident you won't care how much you were paying per month. Your major concern will be, do I have enough coverage?

As your agent John I never want to have that 3am phone call where you call me telling me...

So, what you'll find is that although my process is somewhat detailed at the end of it you'll be much more comfortable knowing you made the correct insurance purchase.

The most important expectation to set is that insurance is for the big things. Insurance is not well built for minor damage it's meant for major claims and major accidents.

Speaking in the future tense is a great way to plant seeds. There are two types of seeds when selling insurance that we need to plant. We need to plant seeds of fortification and seeds of doubt. Fundamentally at the end of the sales process the insured has to make a decision and arrive a conclusion. They will chose one of two paths:

- I will risk being underinsured and stay with my agent.

- I will sign up with this new agent and new insurance.

*"Whatever you are, be a good one."* –
Abraham Lincoln

## Chapter 3: Identify Weaknesses and Gaps in current offer.

Product comparison is your best friend in the insurance industry. If we can identify gaps and weaknesses that might become a large problem for a client, then we can tailor a solution. The client has to agree there is a problem before we can pitch a solution.

Let's talk a little about how to show a client that you care. It's really easy to show a client that their current agent or broker doesn't care. If they did they wouldn't put you in a situation to lose your assets or have these gaps. (This is a training facing statement not client facing statement.) But, to show someone you care take the time to understand them as a prospect not just understand the Dec Page.

## Problem Identification

The center piece of selling and marketing is problem identification. We need to uncover a problem and discover a solution to fulfill that problem. Do you ever ask yourself why people sit in front of you? Because, they have an unmet need or a curiosity if you could solve a problem. Most agents misdiagnose the problem. Most consumers now a days come into your office and think what? Consumers think that because a Lizard on Television told them they could save 99% on their insurance that they're overpaying, when in fact most people are underpaying (because of being underinsured). Eighty percent of consumers shop based on price, because they see price as a problem. Why? Because, with your insurance you don't know what you have until you have the misfortune of actually having to use it. Our job is to shift the focus from price to value. Our job is to shift the conversation to protection for the price.

## Upselling Water-Backup Sewer and Drainage

**Question to open:** "As I'm putting these options together would you mind if we looked at sewer and drainage coverage?"

John I don't see water back up and sewer coverage on your policy, have you heard of it? Do you know if your agent put in on?

**Educate:** Do you ever go on vacation? Everyone says yes. Well, what I mean is do you ever go on vacation and leave your air conditioning on if no one is going to be home? Everyone always says no. Let's talk about water back up and sewer coverage, which is not currently on your policy.

**Recommendation:** Based on your needs as your agent I'd recommend being protected with at least the average claims severity for one of these claims which is BLANK.

**Question to close:** "Is that something you would want you're on your policy?"

Transitioning Questions
- Would the client consider paying a little but more to put all of this policies with the same company or to get better coverage?
- Do you want to be covered for major accidents or major claims?

Don't make up a prospects mind for them.

Don't assume what someone can and cannot afford. Don't assume that someone because of their existing limits is not an umbrella candidate or doesn't value insurance. People will tell you what they value and what they do not value. The biggest mistake most agents make is doing just that. A Dec page doesn't tell me much about a client. It doesn't tell me what they care about.

### Inferring Micro Agreements

What I found to be most effective for upselling was getting numerous periodic 'yes' responses during the process. This would allow me to judge rapport during the process as well. So, when picking apart a current offering the best way is to not tell the person they don't carry enough insurance, but asking if they want the coverage. Also, ask open ended questions to get them thinking differently about insurance.

- "Have you thought about adding on Sewer Back Up coverage?"

- "Are you okay with not having coverage for major losses?"

## The Goal of a Sales Person

Our main goal is to properly insure the risk. If we can expose weaknesses and address concerns, we can start to shift the focus from price to value. Ultimately the decision rests in the hands of the consumer to purchase the insurance that suits their needs. The endorsements I'll talk about in this book are endorsements that usually are rarely addressed, but our well designed by the insurance companies and ISO.

## Typical Weaknesses

Your typical weaknesses on an auto policy:

- Liability Limits
- Med Pay
- Rental Car
- Deductible Waiver
- UMBI Lower than BI Limits
- Low Deductibles

Your typical weaknesses on a home insurance policy:

- Low Liability
- Wrong Replacement Cost
- No Inflation Rider
- No Extended Replacement Cost
- No Water-backup coverage
- Low Med Pay
- No Wedding Ring Endorsed
- No discussion of Fair Rental Value

"True friendship is a plant of slow growth, and must undergo and withstand the shocks of adversity, before it is entitled to the appellation." - George Washington

## Chapter 4: Customize a solution based on that information.

When you customize a solution the consumer has to agree there is a problem and that they want to purchase the solution. For instance, a lot of Agents tell consumers that, "You need an Umbrella policy or you need earthquake insurance..."

We get so ingrained sometimes in our own work that we forget to ask questions and forget to help educate the consumer on their actual needs. We as Agents know that someone needs an umbrella policy, but us just knowing that doesn't help a consumer understand why they really need one.

When do you explain the coverage to the insured? How do you explain the coverage to the insured? Where in the sales process do you find it most effective? For me it depends on who the person is and how much time I have with the person. If I can do a fact finding meeting and then a separate presentation meeting that is most effective.

Explain the coverage line by line.

When you explain the coverage to the consumer remember that they have very little experience with insurance. The consumer most likely doesn't understand what they have or what they need. The more you can focus on education during your process the better. Explain the coverage in simple terms. By explaining coverage we by design are shifting focus from price to coverage or from price to perceived value. The question the consumer will start asking in their head is not what am I going to pay, but what am I really paying for (now)? Explain the coverage line by line and learn where to spend time.

## Explain the Endorsements

We had a lead come in one day. By looking at the Dec page we thought it was a normal home insurance policy. As we started talking we learned they were running a day care out of the home. Endorsements are your best friend when it comes to acquiring new business if you don't plan on selling on price. Insurance companies spent a lot of giving you the tools to customize an insurance policy. Learn the endorsements and use them accordingly.

## Checking Rapport

Think of checking rapport like cooking a turkey. Selling insurance is a process much like cooking a turkey. You have to thaw the turkey for a certain amount of hours. You have to preheat the oven, you have to baste the turkey, you have to garnish it and stick it in the oven. If you stick it in before the oven has reached it's preheated optimal temp then you are going to ruin your turkey. But, every so often you need to check the internal temperature before pulling it out completely.

Rapport building should be done in a similar fashion as checking the turkey. You don't build rapport a single time in the beginning of the sales process and then never again. You need to check it. "How does all this sound so far John?" Or, "John does this all make sense so far?" What you are doing is building affirmation along the road to the close but also checking to see if the person is grasping what you are saying. We have some more specific examples later on in this book.

Put the power in the hands of the consumer.

Remember we are giving them something to think about not telling them how or what to think.

- Is that something you would like to be covered for?
- Is that something you want on your policy?

### Who is in the home?

Remember when we asked this question during the first part of the process? We did that to understand the risk and help us customize the policy. Is there a spouse? A grandparent? What is the policy definition for "Family Member" in the home? When does regular usage cross over from permissive use driving? When is a dwelling a seasonable dwelling? Is one of the rooms being rented out? All these questions we need to know the answers to.

## Leveraging Fair Rental Value

One completely overlooked policy feature for some companies is the loss of use feature known as Fair Rental Value. Some policies have this and some do not. For instance, if you are renting out part of your home and the home burns down forcing the renter out of the home or forcing you to lose out on rental income, some policies will cover this under a home owners policy form. This is a policy feature that people care about, if they have a renter.

## Closing the Show.

After you have gone through all of this leg work you need to close the show. Just ask for the sale. John, this is the policy you need to protect your family, how would you like to pay? And shut up. The beauty in doing that much front loaded work is you've answered most of the objections through the classification process and gotten them to take price off the table within reason. Just sit back and listen. Remember the person who cares least wins. So, sometimes I would just hand them the Dec Page ask for the sale and then start doodling on some paper. Silence can be your best friend during the close. You've done everything right. You've explained everything in detail, you've addressed all the concerns, you've filled the gaps, and now just see what the response is. Don't overcomplicate it.

"Didn't make sense not to live for fun. Your brain gets smart but your head gets dumb." – Smash Mouth

## Chapter 5: Auto Insurance Case Study

Let's say a prospect walks in and provides this Dec page and asks you for a quote. This Dec page will mean many things to many different people. (See below)

### Coverages

| Coverages | Limits or Deductibles | 2013 HYUND ELANTRA GS |
|---|---|---|
| Liability | 100,000/300,000 | $643.00 |
| Property Damage | 50,000 | $245.00 |
| Uninsd/Underinsd Motorists | 100,000/300,000 | $104.00 |
| Medical Payments | 5,000 | $116.00 |
| Comprehensive | 1,000 | $72.00 |
| Collision | 1,000 | $376.00 |
| TOTAL PER VEHICLE | | $1,556.00 |

What are your initial thoughts when reviewing this policy?

_____

_____

_____
_____
_____
_____
_____.

Does this client have enough insurance in California?

No, they do not. If you think that might be adequate coverage, would you write this policy for yourself? Better yet. Would you write this policy for your mother? Exactly. Enough said.

What did the agent do right?

The deductibles are in a competitive sweet spot and good for the insured/insurance company and insurance agency. Also, the limits are at least above state minimum.

How do we know if a client has enough insurance? Do the math.

| Limits | AVERAGE JURY AWARD IN CA | What you owe. |
|---|---|---|
| 15,000 | $506,070 | ($491,070) |
| 100,000 | $506,070 | ($406,070) |
| 250,000 | $506,070 | ($256,070) |
| What the insurance company pays. | | What you owe. |
| Plantiffs win 41% of the time. | | |
| In CA over 250,000 people go bankrupt every year. | | |

Above is a simple way to upsell limits for the prospects you have determined as 'think' people. Just go over the numbers. In the state of California the average jury award for personal injury is now above $500,000. So, one way to sell liability is this simple. For instance, hand the client a calculator and have them type in $506,070. Do me a favor and type that into the calculator. Now do me another favor can you subtract your liability limit of $100,000. What does that come out to? $406,070... In the event you are involved in a major accident your deductible just went from $1000 to $406,070.

Depending on the response you get you can then pivot or transition to umbrella insurance. The one question you always have to ask is, "Is the client asking buying questions or do they need more to think about?"

### Two Facts for Liability Coverage
- In CA about 41% of plaintiffs win.

- In CA about 1 person declares bankruptcy every minute.

*But, Mike I don't drive much anymore...*

John, to be honest I don't drive much either anymore. Last week I was involved in an accident and sideswiped by a driver with no insurance. It happened about 2 minutes from my house.

John, lemme ask you something. Would you be surprised to know that about 90% of accidents happen within 25 miles of your home? Why is that? Most things we do are close to home. You are the most comfortable when you are close to home. Frankly, our guard drops a little bit.

*Addressing Property Damage*

Why is $50,000 a low limit? The <u>average</u>

automobile is $30,000 brand new. What if you hit a light pole? That's $10,000 to $20,000. Just use facts and figures and questions. We had a client hit a light pole, how much would you think it would cost to replace if you hit one? I'm always surprised by the answers because they usually have a wide range.

Let me ask you something as a reader. Let's say you get into an accident. How many cars do you plan on hitting? How many objects? How many people are in those cars? How much property are those cares carrying?

The average property damage claim severity in the US is relatively low for the most part. The reason why it is low is the fact we have a high frequency that drags down the average claim. So, then why should we upsell higher limits? Because, insurance is about procuring peace of mind. If you get into a major accident or hit multiple vehicles, good luck.

Think about it as an Agent. What kind of car do you drive? What kind of cars do you see driving on the freeway? Look to your left there's a Mercedes, to your right a Maserati, behind you maybe a Lexus...

### Common Mistakes Agents Make

Believe it or not. I've heard agents say not everyone needs an umbrella policy. What??? If you work or have assets you need to have an umbrella. Common mistakes:

- Different BI vs UMBI limits
- Low Deductibles
- Low Medical Payments
- Waiver of Deductible (Missing)
- Parked Car Collision (Missing)

Let's tackle all of these one by one. Why would you sell your client low UMBI? Because, you do not understand how it works. Believe it or not. I've also heard an agent tell a prospect that if they have health insurance they do not need a lot of UMBI.... What??? That's like saying most Agent's do not need E&O because they can get on a plane to Argentina if they get sued by a client. UMBI is the most important coverage on the policy. It's the part the actual insured uses, it's a first party coverage.

Low deductibles are traps for your preferred clients. Why? Because, the more you use your insurance the worse your life becomes financially. About 3-5% of your customers are going to use their auto insurance every year. It's a rather low number for the most part. Although for the purposes of subrogation it is sometimes advantageous to have medium or low deductibles. For the purposes of having good rates, you don't want to use your insurance unless you really have to. Again, these are first party coverages. My grandmother was the first female claims manager for a very large insurance company. She always told me from a young age, "You never use your insurance unless you absolutely have to."

Low Medical payment coverage always drives me a little bit bonkers because this is a 1st party coverage for you or people in your vehicle. If you are injured in an auto accident this is one of the most important coverages to help ease the physical and financial pain.

### Selling Medical Payments Coverage

Medical Payments Auto: "We will pay reasonable expenses incurred for necessary medical and funeral services to or for an "insured" who sustains "bodily injury" caused by "accident". We will pay only those expenses incurred, for services rendered within three years from the date of the "accident"."

Question to open.

- John, I don't see probably the most important coverage on your dec page, Med Pay, do you know if you have it?

- John, would you mind if we took some time to talk about one of the most important coverages on your auto insurance, med pay?

- John would it be okay if we spent a little bit of time to talk about Med Pay Coverage?

- Have you heard of Med Pay coverage?

- In the event you are crossing the street and someone hits you, would you want some help with the medical bills?

- In the event you are riding your bike and someone hits you, would you want some help paying the medical bills?

## Educate

Medical Payments coverage covers you or passengers in the event of an accident. Often your health insurance has a high deductible.

What's your health insurance deductible? Mine's almost $7000 of out of pocket cost.

In an auto accident, if you have to take an ambulance to the hospital how much do you think that ambulance ride costs?

Unfortunately, that $2000 ambulance ride is not covered currently under your policy. What Is your health insurance deductible set at? $2000, $3000, $4000, $50000? In the event of an accident those medical costs you incurred would be covered under your medical payments coverage. It's basically there to fill in the gaps your health insurance won't cover during an accident.

This is where you can put in a personal or

client story on how the coverage works.

### Recommendation

As your agent, I'd recommend getting at least blank amount of coverage.

### Question to Close

- Is that something you want on your policy?

- Is that something you want protection for?

- Is that something you want?

*"Genius is one percent inspiration and ninety-nine percent perspiration."* – Thomas Edison

## Chapter 6: Home Insurance Case Study

A client walks into your office and presents this Dec page. Before the client evens open their mouth you immediately have gathered some information. But, not enough information to help them make an informed decision. (See Below)

| Coverage | Limits of Liability | Premium |
|---|---|---|
| Total Policy Premium | | $749 |
| Section I - Property Protection | | |
| Cov A - Dwelling | 500,000 | 650 |
| Cov B - Other Structures | 50,000 | 50 |
| Cov C - Personal Property | 350,000 | |
| Cov D - Loss of Use | 100,000 or 12 months | |
| Deductible - All Perils | 1000 | |
| | | |
| Section II - Liability | | |
| Cov E - Liability | 100,000 | 40 |
| Cov F - Medical Payments to Others | 2,000 | 9 |

What are your initial thoughts after reviewing this policy?

_____

_____

_____
_____
_____
_____
_____.

Q: Does the client have proper limits? Yes, No or Maybe

A: Maybe, it's hard to say without running the replacement cost and then digging.

Q: What does the client care about?_____

A: Hard to say. This looks somewhat generic.

Q: Is the client properly insured? Yes, No or Maybe.

A: No. We can for sure see that there are lower limits and missing endorsements.

Q: Did their current agent do a good job? Yes, No or Maybe.

A: Most likely not.

When I look at the above Dec page here is what I see...

1. Low liability limit.
2. Low medical payments.
3. I don't see an endorsed wedding ring.
4. I don't see extended replacement cost.
5. The consumer wasn't sold an umbrella policy most likely.
6. The deductible is low.
7. I don't see Water-Back Up sewer and drainage endorsed.
8. Errors and Omission's claims...

$1000 vs $2500 on a home deductible.

Most agents really drop the ball when it

comes to deductibles. You ever hear this one, "Well, why should I bump up the client's deductible?" He is only paying $749 and that would be an increase of 1500 if he had a claim... Insurance is for the big stuff. The major claims. It's not a maintenance policy. It's not a warranty policy. When I sell a deductible it's with in mind that the claim is to replace the home. Not to replace a broken window. If we can lower the premium and use the savings to sell the increased endorsements then it's a win-win-win. The insurance company gets a higher SIR, which means lower claims frequency and lower severity. The customer get more coverage for around the same price and the agent gets a higher chance at hitting his or her profit bonus.

How you ask the question normally determines the response you receive. For instance, "Have you thought about increasing your deductible?"

Where is the reason? Where is the why? What real reason is there for me doing this? Don't just make blind recommendations to make recommendations. I see this problem a lot with Agents recommending umbrella insurance. "Well, because you own a home and have assets you should buy an umbrella..." Wrong.

Instead why not try this...

"Hey John, your deductible is kind of low you could probably save a considerable amount of money if you increased it. Have you thought about increasing your deductible?" (I only used this depending on the relationship to the prospect and rapport)

John: Not really. That's kind of a big increase.

Agent: John lemme ask you something. If your home burned to the ground in a fire.

Could you find $2500 to rebuild it? (What do you think the response is?) 99% of the time I received a yes answer to this question.

### Upselling Low Liability Limits

Is having a $100,000 liability limit on a $500,000 home responsible? Intuitively you know the answer. The answer is no. Because, if heaven forbid you become entangled into a lawsuit that is the first asset the lawyer will come after.

John, lemme ask you something. If you were to guess, how large do you think the average jury award is for someone who gets injured on your property? In other words, someone slips and falls on your property, how much do you think the jury will award that person for injuries... on average?

Believe it or not the average jury award in the state of California is **$699,489**...

Most claims have a somewhat low severity for liability. But, insurance is for the big things, the major claims. When a claim goes to court you end up paying big time.

So, what are your most common liability claims?

- Dog Bites
- Home Accidents
- Falling Trees
- Drunk Guests
- Injured Domestic Workers

Remember an insurance company is a business. If you severely damage someone else's property, injure someone (BI) or slander (PI) someone and it goes to court, the insurance company will cut a check for your limit and run for the hills. As an Agent we are selling peace of mind. If your insurance doesn't cover the major claims the catastrophic liability claims, then what are you really buying?

## Jewelry Sublimit

When I train groups of Agents. I always like to ask this question. What do you think the most valuable item every person usually wears? A wedding ring. So naturally my next question is, then why isn't on your clients home policy? About 5% of policies that come across your desk probably have a ring on it. The sublimit on Jewelry is $1500. Most women own that in cosmetic jewelry alone. Whenever I start picking apart a policy this is the first gap I uncover and for this reason I always prefer having both spouses at the presentation.

## Low Medical Payments to Guests/Others

What does this coverage do? It's a no

fault coverage for people who become injured on your property. For instance, we had a wedding at our house and one of our guests slipped on a stair case and had some minor injuries. We used our medical payments to help her out with her bills after she went to the urgent care to get checked out. Medical payment coverage is not saying we are at fault or accepting liability for someone else's injuries, what is says is please do not take me to court or seek out a personal injury attorney. Look there are about 20,000,000 million injuries on residences per year and over $240,000,000,000 in damages. You can't upsell $1,000 to $10,000 of Med Pay? What's the difference in premium, $25 per year?

## Extended Replacement Cost Coverage

If this endorsement is not on a policy then you are not insuring your clients correctly. Why? This is when you have the delicate conversation of demand surge. First what makes a reconstruction cost...

| Material Costs | $200,000.00 | 40% |
| Other Costs | $25,000.00 | 5% |
| Labor Cost | $150,000.00 | 30% |
| Profit Margin | $75,000.00 | 15% |
| Permits and Legal | $50,000.00 | 10% |
| Total Replacement Cost | $500,000.00 | 100% |

Each time you run a replacement cost calculator print it out and there should be a simple breakdown like this with percentages. Make sure to attach it to the signed application for E&O purposes. (The above averages are not accurate)

Current RCT vs Policy Written RCT.

What I've found is that most policies that will come across your desk are grossly underinsured for the current risk. A lot of agents use these cute little tricks like under-insuring the home and then adding an extended RC endorsement, because the cost of insurance for the difference is more affordable than properly insuring the home. Brilliant I know...

## Demand Surge and the RCT

What is Demand Surge? When your home burns down. It will cost X to replace. The RCT calculates into it the cost of labor and materials as the primary cost. There are only so many trees that can be cut down and so many contractors that can operate in an area. Contractors don't grow on trees. But, what happens when an entire neighborhood burns down? The price of labor goes up and the price of materials goes up. The government takes longer to process paperwork because the demand now has increased. This is what we call Demand Surge and believe it or not the price of labor can increase by 10 to 20%. This is why having a Blanket Protection limit or

Extended Replacement cost is a must for home insurance. We never sold a policy without one of the two.

"Change your thoughts and you change your world." - *Norman Vincent Peale*

## Chapter 7: Mindset

Having the right mindset will help you thru the hard times. Most people forget that perception is reality. If you only think about price and you think the client only thinks about price, where does the conversation steer? If you think insurance has become commoditize and your only value is price shopping, where do you think the conversation will go?

Selling is the ultimate test of your endurance. More so than any endeavor in your life. Selling tests the boundaries of your pain threshold and your imagination. Your capacity to endure these challenges is what will separate you from the rest. The easy way out is to say, "We are just not competitive." There will always be a more competitive insurance company, find what makes yours a good for the client. Whenever I get that objection, I always start by asking to look at a Dec Page they are going up against. And then we just start picking it a part or I pick apart what the Agent quoted.

Although we have talked throughout my books about how to develop systems and closing techniques, we do touch a lot on the intangibles. The intangibles all sales people have to consider; motivation, hope, inspiration and dealing with fear.

What if this person says no? What if they say yes? What if I become hugely successful and can't handle it? What if I don't and become a failure? The overarching narrative of all of my books is this one simple thought. **Everything in the sales process is more or less within your control.** Your mindset and your vision is what will help you through the hard times. Hard times will come for everyone. Sometimes you sell 100 policies in a month and the next you can't close a prospect to save your life.

Have you ever heard the statement,

"Sometimes I'll do it later often becomes I'll do it never." Think about that for a second. Have you yourself ever fallen into this trap? If only I had a more competitive insurance company. If only I had more time. If only I had more staff I would sell more.

## Me, Myself and I

In 2016, after selling my book of business I decided to remove social media from my phone. Over the next two years I found that I had unlocked a veritable treasure trove of productivity. Why? Because, I was to externally focused on what others were doing and where people were going to take food selfies. Top Producers in any industry focus on themselves and building their craft. In your practice focus on the client, in your downtime focus on yourself. *As an aside the most successful people rarely ever brag about their success on social media.*

*"Prospecting is about seeing enough people and saying the right things to those people." –  Old Selling Proverb*

## Chapter 8: Goal Setting

Goal setting is great if you have a barometer. If you start from scratch don't focus too much on goals. Focus more on creating a vision and focus on activities that will drive results. Activities and behaviors drive results, setting goals is meaningless in a vacuum that doesn't include activity.

Eventually you will become busy to the point to where you need to scale your practice and hire. But, you can set goals all day until the cows come home and it won't get you one step closer to achieving those goals.

Goal Setting Example (Reverse Sales Funnel)

- You set a goal of making $5,000 this month from P&C sales.

- You need to write 50 policies as your average client is $1000 in premium and you make 10% commission.

- You close 50% of your presentations so now you need to present to 100 people.

- 75% of people show up to your presentations so you need to set up 133 appointments.

- You work 5 days a week so you need to schedule for 6 presentations per day.

- I can convert 10% of people I speak with into setting an appointment. So I need to speak to 1330 per month to meet my goal, assuming those are mostly strangers or cold leads.

The real question is how do you plan on finding people to set up presentations and appointments? Number crunching and goal setting becomes somewhat end in itself not a means to an end.

When you create a vision, what you are creating is a powerful tool for self-motivation. A vision has a 'why' attached to it. There is a reason why you want to achieve something. A goal is more a place holder because in theory the goal should always increase. A vision is more of a state you want to actualize. Ask yourself when you set up a goal or a vision. Why is this important to me? Is it important to me? What does this mean if I achieve that? Is it a must or a should? What do you want to represent? What do you stand for?

When you start off creating your goals. Be conservative and make sure they are reasonable and rooted in the real world. I'm not saying to not aim for the stars, but the first rocket didn't reach the moon.

'My first month as an Agent I want to write 40 policies...'

- Do you have the marketing funnel established to meet these goals?

- Is it a stretch goal or a realistic goal?
- Do you have the established pipeline to achieve this?

I'm a strong believer in incrementalism when establishing goals and in life. This week what do you want to accomplish and achieve? Start from that mindset.

### Vision

People often confuse having a vision with having a goal. A goal is a means to an end and a vision is the idealism state of being at the end of the rainbow. A vision is meant to be lofty, goals are milestones that should be achievable.

*"Opportunities don't happen. You create them."* -- Chris Grosser

## Chapter 09: Closing

### My thoughts on Closing

Closing should be the easiest part of the process, if I did my job correctly. Why? Because, selling isn't about a back and forth of competing efforts. Selling is a collaborative experience, which involves the sharing of ideas and reciprocity. Selling is a search for the truth. Closing shouldn't take up al of time or occupy a lot of your conversation. Closing should be the quickest, easiest and most painless part of the process.

I was never a 'hard close' kind of guy. Trying to negotiate and convince somebody they are wrong is about as easy of a task as pushing rope. As you progress through the sale micro-closes are what it takes to tip the scales of persuasion. Get the client to agree to concepts, features and benefits, not just a price.

## Closing Strategies

As a strategy we can either go for hard closes and negotiating or we can go with Soft Closes. Micro Closes.

## Closing Statements

Closing statements short be short and to the point. I've made my professional recommendation and spent the time to educate your about your needs. Along with that we have spent time to build customized solutions to fulfill those needs.

- How would you like to pay?

## Stop, Look and Listen...

There's this old song from the 70's called 'Stop, Look, Listen..." This is how we close. We ask for the sale, shut up and listen. Remember, we have two ears and one mouth for a reason, take that ratio into account when closing a sale.

*"Success is not final; failure is not fatal: It is the courage to continue that counts."*--
Winston S. Churchill

## Chapter 10: Objections

There is no one size fits all approach to handling every objection in every situation. What might help is understanding why people object, when, how and what they say. Developing a framework is for objection handling is more important than lazily putting together a bunch of rebuttals and hoping for the best.

What is an objection? An **Objection** is an expression or feeling of disapproval or opposition; a reason for disagreeing. Objections are basically an evolutionary defense mechanism consumers use to stall for time or alleviate tension during a sales situation or use as an exit.

### Types of Objections

All objections basically fall into the same four categories. Either a client has:

- No Time (Sense of urgency)
- No Money (Lack of Value)
- No Need/Want (No interest)
- No Trust (Uncertainty about Company, Product or You)

## No Time

If a client tells you they do not have time, either they do not have time or they don't feel a need to get it down right now. What it really comes down to is a lack of urgency.

## No Money

If a client provides you with a price based objection, they either genuinely cannot afford the product and or they do not see the value.

## No Need

This is another objection that stems from lack of qualified prospects and or they don't see how it applies to them specifically. Lack of problem identification and or qualification.

## No Trust

If a client has no trust, then you either skipped rapport building, neglected to provide credible information or clarification about your company, product/service and or you.

## Rebuttals

Here's the thing about rebuttals, not everyone is a client. You can be a slick as a bowling alley, but that doesn't mean you'll close every case. People are going to say no, what I can say is don't burn the relationship bridge. Follow up is half the game of sales, try not to push people over the edge.

- There is no such thing as a good deal for the wrong insurance policy.
- Would you feel safe purchasing a car knowing it had a faulty airbag?
- It's called umbrella insurance because like an umbrella I'd rather have one and not need it then need one and not have one.
- It really does me no good to sell you a policy that does you no good.

## Why do people object?

Why do you think people object? Objections are par for the course, but why do you think people object? In my approximation people object for the following reasons:

- We confused the prospect.

- The Prospect is not qualified.

- We didn't answer a question.

- We didn't address a concern.

- Lack of explanation of concepts.

- We talked our self out of a sale (Didn't listen to buying signals)

- Lack of certainty

- Lack of trust

## Complaint vs Objection

I come from a big Italian family, arguing and complaining are the centerpieces of any family dinner. When dealing with clients it's important to understand that sometimes people just like to complain. Sometimes a complaint seems and feels like an objection.

Flight, Fight or Freeze

Animals have three options when faced with adversary. We can run, we can fight and or we can freeze. Objections are basically a way of giving the client a way to do any three of the things.

"The perennial student is the richest person on earth." –Michael Bonilla

## Chapter 11: Sales Rules/Tips

### Rule Number 1: Don't Complicate Something Simple.

Rule number one of selling insurance is to keep it simple and to the point. We are selling insurance not building a space ship. Most consumers don't know what they don't know. Most consumers don't know what they have, what they need, what they're current risk profile looks like and what they are missing out on. Explain the concepts in digestible terms that consumers can actually understand and stray away from using too much insurance jargon.

About 5 years ago or so, I had the misfortune of sitting through a long-winded sales consultation with a life agent appointed by one of the world's largest life insurance companies. The life agent had a well thought out, but thoroughly confusing Indexed Universal Life Presentation. After about 45 minutes of this life rep carrying on I started wondering if she actually was going to stop talking and listen.

Rule Number 2: Always be agreeable.

Selling is as much an art as it is a science. There is no formula for agreeableness, some people are naturally more agreeable than others. Just know that the more confrontational we are as salespeople the worse your odds are for closing a sale. The first person to agree is generally the one that is going to have the advantage during the negotiating process. When we agree we are changing the language of the typical sales process, in that, this is not going to be an 'I'm right and you're wrong' type of conversation. This conversation is going to be a collaborative experience.

Rule Number 3: Understand the Person.

Don't make snap judgements about what someone can afford. Dig. Take the time to ask questions and understand the person sitting across the table. One day a 'surfer dude' walked into my office, dressed in shorts, a Tommy B shirt, shades on the back of his head, tattered sandals and enough wrist bands to make Johnny Depp envious. What was he looking for? This surfer dude was looking for auto insurance and brought in his Dec page. Now, what would most people assume at this point? Well, clearly he is a candidate for 15/30 state minimum limits, right? Wrong! Turns out his current Dec page did have 15/30, but I started digging the same way I would have for an advanced markets case.

Turns out this surfer dude, who did in fact surf, was also in need of some better insurance. Great, do you own or rent? Currently, he was renting an apartment. So, tell me about the apartment, to which he replied, it's all right. Okay, what do you do for a living? To which he replied, 'I'm an artist.' When I started digging a little further into what that meant, it turns out to my surprise that this gentleman restored art in the ball park of $7,000,000 to $15,000,000 pieces of classical artwork. All of which he kept in his home. Now, how does a person like this get 15/30? According to the prospect, turned client, no one ever bothered to have the conversation with him. Everyone assumed he needed state minimums because his current Dec page had state minimums.

> Rule Number 4: The Prospect Needs to understand you.

Ask yourself does the prospect have enough information to know, like and trust me? According to Bob Berg all things being equal this is the determining ethos people use for selecting whom to do business with. If not, then you need to build that trust through conversation. Why should this person do business with and not the other guy down the street?

## Rule Number 5: Reciprocity

If an insurance sale is a search for the truth we need to follow the rule of reciprocity. The rule of reciprocity makes the insurance buying process a collaborative effort not a confrontational one. Follow a simple rule of thumb, give before you get.

Remember you make no money until the person signs up with you, so you are educating them for free. This is the key to reciprocity. You ask questions to evoke emotions during the process and client has questions that you answer to provide certainty.

Rule Number 6: Stick to a process.

One of my friends had something in her eye and she kept rubbing it to no avail. I passed onto her a simple process I learned, 'close your eye and drag your find down the top and up the bottom halves of your lids, like a windshield wiper.' It's a process that I learned and actually works rather well. To which she replied, 'you have a process for everything.' That didn't used to be the case, I used to be the sales guy who was all personality and energy. This is an overrated sales style that most novice salespeople cling to.

Every person is different, but every sale is exactly the same. In that, people give you the same responses, the same objections and will follow a path. When you start selling insurance it's important to remember that you have a start, you build rapport, you ask questions that are open ended, you find a problem solution/

## Tension Threshold Principle

Emotional Threshold ('Feel' Person)

Open

Close

Intellectual Threshold (Information Overload / 'Think' Person)

There are two types of people that sit in front of you. There are think type of people and feel type of people. What I mean is that people respond to questions in different ways. Some people say, "I think..." and some people say, "I feel..."

The reason why you need to grasp this concept, is the fact that during a sale we have these invisible boundaries. Emotional or feel people require stories and think people require figures and facts. Not everyone is the same. But, there is a limit for feel people and there is a limit for think people that we have to monitor in the sales process.

Rule Number 7: Know When To Close and Know When to Fold.

Some prospects believe it or not just enjoy talking to sales people and have no intention of buying. Being a salesperson you must think that is somewhat crazy, I did. But, it's true. During your presentation it's important to know when people are giving off buying signals and asking buying questions. Why? Because, that will give you a strong indication of when someone is ready to be closed.

Think of a sale like a Turkey in the oven. First you have to marinate the turkey. Then you preheat the oven. After your prep work is complete and the oven is at the right temperature you put the Turkey in the oven. Some turkeys require more prep work because some are FROZEN and some are fresh. You cook the turkey and check the temperature along the way. But, you have to keep marinating the turkey as it cooks. If the internal temperature is correct after X amount of hours you pull it out and it's moist. If you leave it in too long it dries out or maybe even burns or becomes ruined.

I'll make an effort to dispense with the food analogies for the rest of the book. Think of it this way. Think of it like an index. The

'Closability' index. Some people are easier to close than others and some require a tremendous amount of effort. But, either way the prospect will ask buying questions.

Well, what's a buying question? For instance, "How much does this cost?" If you are not interested in a product you do not ask how much it will cost. Simple.

### Rule Number 8: Ask Open Ended Questions

If you are new to sales or new to insurance. Your best friend is the ability to ask open ended questions and leading questions. Would you mind if we talked about open ended questions? This is a directive question asking for permission to ask a question. How do you feel about annuity sales? What do you think about annuity sales? Whatever the answer always remember to ask follow up questions. You have two ears and one mouth so as a ratio ask too questions before you start to babble on about insurance.

### Rule number 9: Set Expectations

Like in any relationship you need to set boundaries. What should a client come to expect of you? What do you expect of a client? A lot of Agents (including myself) tell a client that they meet with each client once per year to make sure the insurance is current or on target. There is nothing customized about that statement for a client. Instead why not just ask. How often would you like to meet each year to discuss your insurance? Most of my clients find once a year to meet their needs but some prefer a call once a quarter to check in.

Rule Number 10: Don't lose control of the conversation.

Probably the most common challenge for newer agents is not maintaining focus. A prospect is going to focus on price if you let them and it can derail the conversation. Price is merely the cost of value. It's your job to educate and present the value. Remember you are the expert and what you focus on will direct the conversation. Don't avoid talking about price, but at the same time don't rush or lead with price. See Diagram Below.

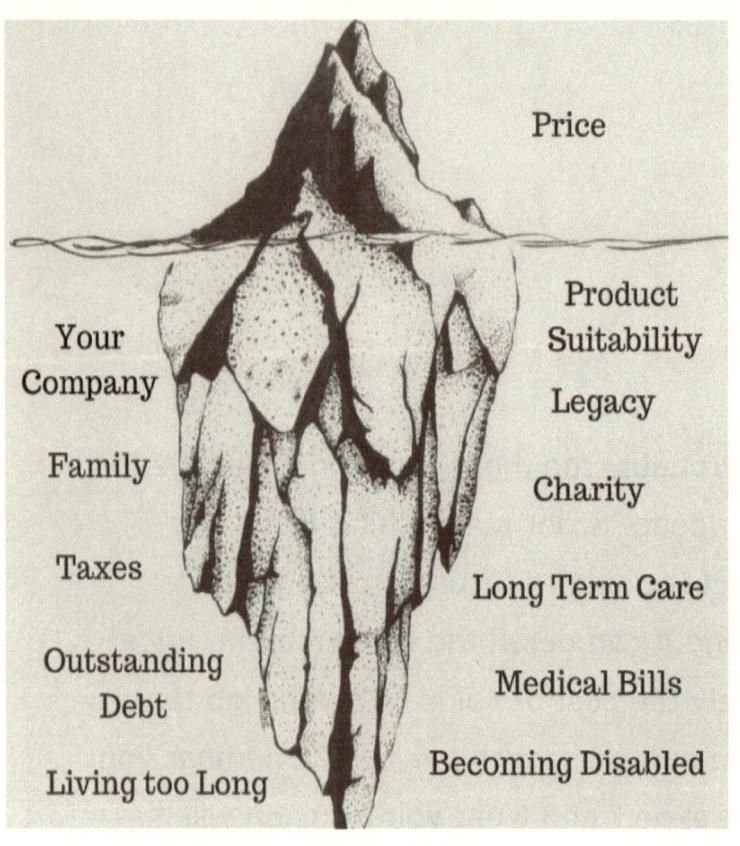

Rule Number 11: Don't always try to reinvent the wheel.

My father was a carpenter and used to say the nail that sticks out tends to get hammered. Craft your approach as you learn your trade. If your trade is selling insurance, then read, apply and learn.

It's important as you craft your style/approach to make adjustments. Somethings might work and somethings might not. But, start by learning from others and adopting an approach and then putting your unique spin on it.

For some people the grass is always greener on the other side of the fence. There are proven systems and sales techniques that you can copy, adopt and emulate. When I first started selling insurance I fell prey to the 'my-way-is-always-better' syndrome, I like to call it learning the hard way.

### Rule Number 12: Speak in Future Tense

Learn to speak in the future tense. As your Agent... fill in the blank statement. While I was going to college I paid my way by being a

Personal Trainer. I learned very quickly to speak in the assumptive future tense. As your blank... here's how I can be of service to you. "Well, I haven't said I would sign up with you yet." This is the response I want to hear from a client, a soft objection or they might ask buying questions and be able to be closed on the spot. I'm planting seeds not seeds of doubt. But, planting a picture in their head to so some thinking. Picturing in their head how working with me is going to look like and benefit them.

## Rule Number 13: Ask for Permission to Ask for the Sale

This is by far my favorite rule and the most overlooked by most insurance salespeople. Along time ago my great grandfather taught me, 'to never open a man's (families) refrigerator without asking for permission.' Why? Because, it's rude among other reasons that might not be as culturally relevant in today's society. When selling make sure to ask for permission to ask for the sale. What I mean is that prior to presenting make sure to ask if it's okay to present a solution. Put some curiosity in there, check the rapport and ask for permission. Don't force your sales pitch on someone.

## Rule Number 14: Don't Present Price Present a Solution.

New salespeople present themselves, because they don't know any better other than to be eager, overzealous, and enthusiastic. Transactional salespeople present on price and only price as the focus. Relationship based salespeople present a product that comes with them as the center piece of value. Consultative sales people present a product and focus on coverage needs. The best salespeople present a solution to a problem and the insurance is vehicle to fulfill the problem/solution dynamic.

> Rule Number 15: Put yourself in a position to win.

Often we try to sell anyone who can fog a mirror. It happens. The hardest lesson to learn as an agent is that not everyone is a customer. People who walk into your office might not be qualified to buy what you are offering. Don't put yourself into a position to fail by trying to qualify and sell everyone. Remember learning about the gold rush? Prospectors sat in rivers sifting through dirt, swirling water in a dish to find flakes of gold. What they were not trying to do was turn that dirt into gold.

## Rule Number 16: Dance through the pain

Persistency is the number one indicator of longevity for a salesperson. Roughly, 97% of life insurance agents and financial advisors fail in the first year. Why? Persistency. We get constantly rejected, again and again. It's not easy to bounce back up and will yourself to keep going.

## Rule Number 17: Have a Personal Story

Having a personal story can make or break your sales presentation. If you don't have a compelling reason for doing what you do, sales becomes infinitely more challenging. After witnessing the 'great recession' I had family members lose 50% of their 401k's and qualified plans, almost overnight. What would have happened if they took immediate annuities on their 401k's? They wouldn't have lost a dime. Now granted a lot of that value was regained, but it took 10 years! Imagine waiting to liquidate your life savings for ten years into your retirement.

## Index of Questions

1. Have you ever considered paying for your insurance in full?
2. How can we help?
3. What brings you by today?
4. Thanks for stopping by, what's on your mind?
5. Before we get started what kind of questions and concerns do you have?
6. When was the last time they sat down with their agent and discussed their needs?
7. How did you hear about us?
8. Oh by the way John who referred you?
9. What do you care about? (with insurance)
10. What else do you care about besides price?
11. Why are you looking for new insurance?

12. Will I get a fair price for what I need? (Price)

13. Will I have enough coverage to protect my family? (Coverage)

14. Will the insurance company pay my claim? (Claims)

15. Have you ever had to use your insurance?

16. Has anyone sat down and explained you how your coverage is supposed to work?

17. When was the last time?

18. What do you do for a living or hobby?

19. How long have you been doing that?

20. How did you get into that?

21. What do you do really well?

**Summation**

Thanks for taking the time to read my book! If you happened to enjoy it, please leave a review or check out some of my other books. Selling insurance isn't an easy task, it takes hard work and dedication. What did you find useful in this presentation? Did you fins all, some or none? Either way, take the time to reflect on what you learned. Use what you found useful, adapt it, or discard it.

## Other Books

**How to Sell Indexed Universal Life Insurance: Using a Supplemental Life Insurance Retirement Plan.** Paperback – February 19, 2018

**How to Sell Annuities: Annuity Sales Techniques, Tips and Strategies.**

How to Sell Life Insurance.: Life Insurance Selling Techniques, Tips and Strategies Jan 27, 2018

How to Sell Property and Casualty Insurance.: Understanding Insurance Sales, Tips and Techniques. Feb 3, 2018

How to Sell Indexed Universal Life Insurance. : Using a Supplemental Life Insurance Retirement Plan. Second Edition Dec 8, 2018

How to sell Annuities. Second Edition: Annuity Sales Techniques, Tips and Strategies. Jan 13, 2019

The Great American Protection Crisis of 2034: Pension Maximization Using an Indexed Universal Life Policy May 31, 2018

How to Start and Build an Insurance Agency. Edition 2: An Insurance Agency and Brokerage Guidebook. Jul 31, 2018

"I only smoke when I drink...": Easy ways to have hard conversations as a life agent. Jan 2, 2019

How to Sell Indexed Universal Life Insurance.: Using a Supplemental Life Insurance Retirement Plan. Second Edition Dec 9, 2018

How to Sell Auto and Home Insurance: A guide to Qualifying and Presenting. Mar 25, 2018

How to Start and Build an Insurance Agency. Edition 2: An Insurance Agency and Brokerage Guidebook. Jul 30, 2018

How to Sell Umbrella Insurance 2nd Edition: A guide to qualify, present and close. Jan 15,

2019

How to Sell Umbrella Insurance.: A guide to Qualify, Present and Close. Mar 18, 2018

How to Start and Build an Insurance Agency: An Insurance Agency and Brokerage Guidebook Mar 28, 2018

How to Market a Modern Insurance Agency.: New School and Old School Marketing Systems. Apr 29, 2018

www.ingramcontent.com/pod-product-compliance
Lightning Source LLC
Chambersburg PA
CBHW030643220526
45463CB00004B/1621